Language Arts/Drama
Grades 5 and up

CREATIVE DRAMA

Great Ideas for Improvisation & Mime

By Mary Brooks

Published by Educational Impressions, Inc.

TITLE
Book Name: Creative Drama

AUTHOR
Mary Brooks

ACKNOWLEDGEMENTS
Designer: Rachel Mackay
Illustrator: Geraldine Sloane
Editor: Pauline Scanlan

ISBN Number: 978-1-56644-283-1

Published in 2008 by Educational Impressions, Inc.
Hawthorne, NJ

website: www.edimpressions.com

Printed in the United States of America

CONTENTS

CREATIVE DRAMA

INTRODUCTION

Creative Drama provides non-specialists with an accessible introduction to using improvisation and mime as part of the arts curriculum.

Drama can be one of the most anxiety-producing, and at the same time rewarding, aspects of the creative arts. A feeling of anxiety about drama is often induced by a sense that it might lead to an out of control classroom; but on the whole, when boundaries are clear, structures set in place, and the teacher has plenty of ideas, it can lead to wonderful work which has positive spin-offs for learning and teaching in other areas of the English curriculum.

Drama permeates our everyday lives. It is integral to children's play, and it is evident in the oratory, rituals, ceremony and celebrations of many traditional and contemporary world cultures.

This is a book of ideas. It is up to the teacher to help the student develop them. They are not in any particular order for appropriate age, gender or culture as every student is different in his or her approach to any given situation.

Try doing a topic first as a mime, then adding dialogue—and then vice versa. The possibilities are endless. All you need are the ideas. I would like to reiterate that total concentration is of the utmost importance in improvisation and mime, both on the part of the teacher and student(s).

From the very first time a student creates an improvisation or mime, the cooperation of other students must be encouraged. Too much laughing and interruptions cause a breakdown in concentration, and whereas we all want our students to enjoy their work, they will achieve better results if they are left alone to work the performance through. THEN the teacher and other students can point out weaknesses and applaud strengths. All actors must be given space and silence in which to do their best.

The confidence and enjoyment students derive from such activities are immeasurable. They stimulate imagination, create dialogue and make students aware of conflict and resolution.

I hope you find *Creative Drama* a long-lasting source of inspiration.

WHAT IS IMPROVISATION?

The art of improvisation is one of the most important skills learned by any would-be actor. It dates back to the Greek and Roman plays and forms the roots of the English "Mummer" plays and the Mystery cycle of plays which began in the 13th Century. At that time, the majority of actors could neither read nor write—they knew the story line, but the dialogue was improvised. The well-known Commedia dell'Arte was performed by Italian professional masked actors who improvised on a traditional plot. The main characters were Harlequin, Pulcinella, Pantaloon, and Columbine. The story line was basically the same—the young lovers outwitting the father and the elderly, wealthy suitor—but the dialogue was not written down but improvised at each performance.

Improvisation is now used in an increasing number of classroom situations with students of all ages. In addition to enhancing teaching and learning and encouraging imagination, some teachers have found improvisation (otherwise known as creative drama) useful as a pathway into addressing tensions that contribute to reading problems, speech and language disorders and dealing with antisocial behavior.

The majority of students are capable of creating a situation and acting it out. All they need is the idea, a suggestion, a situation. The intention of this book is to help teachers by providing hundreds of possible situations which can be used to build a multitude of mimes and improvisations.

CREATIVE DRAMA

QUICK IMPROVISATIONS

All of these scenarios require quick thinking and very little preparation time. Photocopy these pages onto card. Then laminate them and cut them into strips. Let students choose. Suitable for individuals and pairs.

- **You have been warned that the ice is thin but you still go skating. HELP!**
- **You are late for school. You have to get your own lunch. You cut the tip off your finger making sandwiches.**
- **You have moved to a new neighborhood. A man knocks at the door when you are alone in the house. He says he is a neighbor. May he come in?**
- **You admire a skirt (or trousers) in a shop. The size is smaller than you take but you try it/them on. You split the seams.**
- **Your uncle has a yacht. He has left it anchored. You decide to have a trial sail. Disaster.**
- **You and a friend go skiing despite an avalanche warning. There is a rumble and the mountainside starts crumbling. Your friend disappears.**
- **Your sister has become engaged. She leaves her ring on the sink. You try it on. The diamond falls out and down the plug-hole.**
- **You have been dared to make a parachute jump. When you do, your chute fails to open.**
- **You are at the beach. It starts to rain. You take shelter in a cave. What is that moving at the back of the cave?**
- **You are in bed reading. You hear a squeaking noise. You go to investigate. Mouse? Rat? Floor board? Something else!**
- **Your aunt arrives at your door. Her face is covered in blood. She looks scared. You are the only one at home.**
- **You wear your brand new jacket to school despite being told not to. When it is time to go home, your jacket is missing.**
- **Your new puppy is not house trained. You leave your homework (assignment) on the floor. When you come back into the room, the puppy has made a mess on it.**
- **Your friend is allergic to bee stings. You go for a picnic together. She gets stung. What will you do?**
- **You decide to have a barbecue. You get everything ready. When your back is turned, a dog steals all the hamburgers. People are arriving.**
- **You go to the beach. Some people have smashed bottles. You cut your foot badly. Will you confront them?**
- **You are in New York. You are terrified of heights but decide to go to the top of the Empire State Building. You look over the side.**
- **You have long hair. You go to the hairdresser for a trim. You are busy reading a magazine. The hairdresser confuses your appointment with another and cuts your hair very short.**

CREATIVE DRAMA

- You are in art class and have made a beautiful sculpture. Suddenly there is an earthquake.
- You are getting out of the bath. There is an electricity outage and you cannot see a thing. You slip on the soap.
- You have not done your homework. You are in class. The teacher asks you to read your essay aloud.
- You and your best friend have a quarrel. You miss the friendship, so you phone and try to make amends.
- You audition for the principal part in a play. You feel the audition went badly. The phone rings.
- You are asleep in bed. There is a massive explosion. A gas pipe has blown up in your street. Some houses are on fire.
- You are in a dancing competition. You are doing very well until you stumble badly.
- You are doing the dishes. You look out of the window and see an escaped elephant eating your cabbages.
- You buy some perfume for your mother. It was on sale. When she opens it, it smells terrible.
- You are exploring an old house with a friend when you suddenly see a dark outline at the top of the stairs.
- You borrow a valuable book from a friend. She calls to collect it but you say you cannot find it. How does she react?
- You are exploring an old tunnel when you hear a train coming towards you.
- You have a new pet mouse. It goes missing.
- You are on a camping holiday in the forest. You wake to find a snake has crept into your sleeping bag with you for warmth.
- It is a beautiful, hot day. You go to the beach to relax. You fall asleep and awake to find your back one gigantic blister.
- You go fishing. You have a strong bite on your line. You start to land it—it is a shark.
- You are at a funeral. Suddenly a little dog comes into the church and starts doing tricks. You get uncontrollable giggles.
- You are playing a game with a friend. You keep losing. You get very cross about this.
- You have a visit from a cousin you do not like. You decide to play a trick on him/her but he/she tells your mother and it backfires.

CREATIVE DRAMA

- You are given a beautiful and expensive antique watch for your birthday. You forget you have it on and go swimming. It is not waterproof.
- Your grandmother shows you her precious porcelain doll. You accidentally drop it.
- Your friend invites you to see her new pet. It is a huge white rat. You are terrified and it bites you.
- You decide to sit in your father's expensive new car. It is parked on a hill. It starts sliding away.
- You decide to take some honey out of your friend's beehive. You are showing off and do not wear gloves. You are badly stung.
- You are floating on a raft. It drifts out to sea when you fall asleep.
- You receive a phone call which is an invitation to a party. You have also recently had a bad argument with your parents.
- There is a power outage. You search for a candle, find one, light it and then accidentally drop it.
- You are reading a book. Your dog keeps jumping up as it wants to go for a walk. Will you give in?
- The mail arrives. There is an exciting letter for you. What action will you take?
- It is pouring rain. You run for the bus. Your case falls open spilling all the contents on the wet pavement.
- You are baby-sitting. You drop some food on the beautiful cream carpet. You try to hide it before anyone notices it.
- Walking home from school, a fire engine whizzes past. You round the corner and see smoke coming from your house. Is your pet safe?
- You are in a shop. You see a customer take something and hide it inside his/her coat. Take action.
- You are so engrossed in your book in the library you do not realize you have been locked in.
- You promised to post an urgent payment for your mother on the way to school. You find it in your pocket a week later.
- You are in the technology room. To make your friends laugh you put an empty metal container on your head. You can't get it off.
- You decide to be helpful and do the laundry. You forget to separate whites from colors. Your new red football shirt has turned all the whites pink!
- You are off to a party in your best clothes when you get a flat tire.

CREATIVE DRAMA

- You find an old recipe book. You decide to try one of the recipes. You get halfway through it before you realize it requires one dozen eggs.
- You are late for an appointment when you come across an accident.
- You are alone in the house. You hear on TV that there is an escaped convict at large. Then there is a loud knock on the door.
- You go to pet day at school. Your pet is a very large, fierce dog. It escapes.
- You buy hot dogs and chips for everyone at the beach. You are walking back when the tray breaks and the contents fall onto the sand. You are not popular!
- You light a fire at the beach for a barbecue. A strong wind springs up and things go very wrong.
- You go skiing for the first time with some posh new friends whom you want to impress. You are scared of heights and terrified of the chairlift.
- You are in the middle of a row of seats at the school play and the play is serious. You suddenly feel sick.
- You sit by someone on a bus and try to start a conversation. You suddenly realize he/she is deaf.
- You see a blind person approaching with a guide dog. It is not well trained and starts to lead the person onto the road. There is a motorcycle screaming towards them.
- You are in a national speech competition. Everybody is expecting you to do well. You stand on the stage at the microphone and your mind goes blank.
- Driving along a deserted road in a fog, you suddenly see a figure loom up on the road, waving its hands.
- You're at the beach with a friend when the Big One strikes—it's an earthquake followed by a tidal wave.
- Money has gone missing at school. Someone accuses you, but you are innocent. You know who took it but also know he/she had an important reason. What should you do?
- Your brother has a new car. You accidentally skid and drive your bike into the side making a big scrape.
- You are performing a solo song at the end-of-year award ceremony. Suddenly you notice that person you've had a crush on is sitting in the front row watching.
- You arrive home and there is a smell of fresh baking. You liberally help yourself. Mother arrives home and is furious. The baking was for visitors.
- You are putting on nail polish. The cat jumps up and sends the contents of the bottle over your parents' new sofa.
- You are a passenger on a luxury liner. Suddenly there is a fire alarm.

CREATIVE DRAMA

- You are at the zoo. You notice that the visitors area is suddenly deserted. You hear the zookeeper calling you through a megaphone, "Don't move!"
- You are at the dentist. There are terrible moaning sounds coming from inside his office.
- When you are visiting a museum, you are looking at an Egyptian sarcophagus when you hear tapping sounds coming from inside it.
- You are in an ice-cream parlor. You order a triple "special" deluxe, then you bump into someone and drop it.
- You are on your way to a European vacation. You get to the airport and realize you have left your passport behind.
- You are at the Art Gallery. There is a very large, very unusual "sculpture" 8 feet high. You gently touch it and the whole thing collapses.
- You are outside a bank getting money from the money machine when you see three masked men run into the bank. They are armed.
- You are watching a baseball game. The person next to you gets hit by the ball.
- You are on a plane. Two people suddenly stand up in the aisle and tell everyone to keep quiet.
- You are on a plane. The person next to you suddenly vomits.
- You are a witch or sorcerer making a special brew. Something goes terribly wrong.
- While walking you see a beautiful red apple hanging over the fence. You pick it and...
- You accidentally listen in on a telephone conversation due to a crossed line. They are talking about YOU.
- You tell your mother you are going out with a gang member.
- You visit a friend who has had an operation to restore his/her sight. Has it worked?
- You are waiting in a line for the last bus. It arrives and is very full. A big, burly character pushes in front of you.
- You are coming home late and sense you are being followed. You reach your front door but where is your key???
- You are cycling along when you see a car knock a child off her/his bike. The car does not stop.
- It is a hot summer's night. You awake and hear a loud, buzzing noise. There is a swarm of wasps hovering outside your open bedroom window.

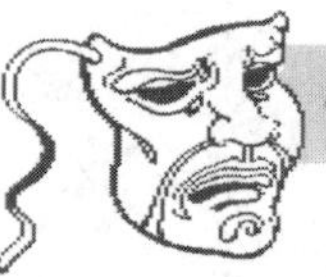

- You are studying for a test. The phone keeps ringing; it is never for you. You become exasperated.
- Walking home you notice something bright red in the sky which suddenly changes color.
- While walking, you hear the cry of an animal in great pain.
- You come across a group of older students bullying a new kid.
- You go into the garden. There is a penguin in your swimming pool.
- You helpfully sweep out the canary's cage for your mother, using the vacuum cleaner. The canary disappears up the hose of the cleaner.
- You go to the Art Gallery. You are looking at the pictures when you see the eyes move in one.
- You are upset to see the dolphins in captivity at Sea World. You plan to help them escape out to sea.
- You brush your teeth. You use shaving cream by mistake.

ONE WORD IMPROVISATIONS

Single words can be used to spark off ideas for improvisations too. These are great because they can be interpreted in so many ways. Cut up the words on the following page and hand them out to small groups. Alternatively, give every one the same word and see how different the interpretations are. You might need to go through the variety of interpretations that a single work can elicit. For example, the word "Loss" might be interpreted as:

Loss of a pet | **Loss of money**

Loss of a game | **Loss of teeth**

Loss of a library book | **Loss of confidence**

Loss of a plane ticket | **Loss of valued object**

Loss of hair (in machine or from illness)

Loss of a grandparent (or other family member)

Loss of a friend (through quarrel or accident)

Loss of an article belonging to someone else

Fear	Leave	Snake	Pain
Happy	Gift	Prison	Distance
Pleasure	Food	Auntie	Letter
Despair	Treasure	Fail	Contempt
Lonely	Fire	Desert	Grief
Heat	Broken	Wait	Smoke
Love	Ice	Impatience	Goodbye
Pride	Thief	Horror	Joy
Journey	Homework	Hate	Secret
Bridesmaid	Disaster	Nightmare	Bicycle
Slyness	Anger	Balloon	Triumph
Bully	Family	Alone	Window
Capsize	Believe	Stupid	Collar
Break	Temple	Crypt	Lie
Birthday	Kiss	Small	Brilliant
Drip	Applause	Clock	Shell

For students who get stuck, you can help them along with prompts for a few of these words. For example:

Fear	**of being left alone; a new school; a dare to stay overnight in a dark house.**
Happy	**an unexpected visit; a gift; high marks; good news; lotto win; a beautiful day at the beach.**
Despair	**of coming to terms with math; sickness of beloved pet; saving enough for a trip; of ever being first.**
Lonely	**new school; boarding school; new neighborhood; new country; left alone in the house; no one to play with on vacation.**
Heat	**cross-country race; on beach; from fire; in jungle.**
Family	**place or role in family; family love; distance from family; pressure of family expectations.**
Joy	**new baby; grandmother's recovery from bad illness; surprise birthday party; new mountain bike, horse, skates, etc.**
Surprise	**visit; gift; party; news; success; holiday.**
Secrets	**being told them; bad or good news; finding a letter; planning a surprise.**
Anger	**cheating; being kept in; not allowed to go to a party; wrongful accusation; someone breaking a possession.**

One-word improvisations might lead to being extended and reaching a dramatic ending, or they might be used for "quick impressions" with the rest of the class trying to guess what the word is. If this is the case, the group should NOT use the word as part of their improvised dialogue.

TWISTS AND TURNS

Life is full of unexpected twists and turns. A simple situation can suddenly turn into a major dramatic incident. A great source for improvisation is the use of the word "WHEN." "Everything is going fine WHEN—" and then it is up to the student to come up with something which occurs which is anything but FINE!

Following are some situations when the use of WHEN can trigger an imaginative response. Try it also as oral improvisation for a warm up. Seat students in a large circle and read these situations. Each student has to answer in turn. No thinking allowed! Extend students' responses by repeating "WHEN" to them as a way of making them continue. Alternate with "AND" from time to time.

CREATIVE DRAMA

WHEN...?

- You are at the top of a tower WHEN
- You are snowboarding WHEN
- You walk on stage to sing your solo WHEN
- You are trying your hand at baking bread WHEN
- You give your teacher your homework WHEN
- You are at the movies WHEN
- You are washing the dishes WHEN
- You are chopping wood WHEN
- You are pushing a carriage across the road WHEN
- You step into space for a bungy jump WHEN
- You are walking through an aquarium WHEN
- You are visiting a crocodile farm WHEN
- You are cycling downhill WHEN
- You are fishing from a small boat WHEN
- You open the fridge door WHEN
- You are out in a canoe WHEN
- You are waiting for a bus WHEN
- You are about to collect the mail WHEN
- You are visiting a sick friend in the hospital WHEN
- You are about to dive into a swimming pool WHEN
- You are taking a shower WHEN
- You are helping in the garden WHEN
- You are just finishing a sculpture in art class WHEN
- You are collecting for the Red Cross WHEN
- You are feeding your new goldfish WHEN
- You are sun-bathing on the beach WHEN
- You are selecting a gift for your mother WHEN
- You are kicking a ball around in the garden WHEN
- You are doing your newspaper route WHEN
- You are playing a tough game of squash WHEN
- You are sent home early from school WHEN
- You are travelling in a coach on a school outing WHEN
- You take your little brother or sister to the park WHEN
- You are on the giant Ferris wheel at a fairground WHEN
- You are washing your hair and reach for the shampoo bottle WHEN
- You walk past a property which is the home of a fierce dog WHEN
- You are brushing your teeth with an electric toothbrush WHEN
- You are roller-blading down the middle of the road WHEN
- You climb the steps in the library to fetch a book WHEN
- You are trying to find a seat in the dark in a cinema WHEN

BUILDING DIALOGUE

Improvising dialogue can be a challenge for many students. Try these exchanges and first and last lines of a dialogue as a way of building up confidence in the spoken word.

- Divide the class into pairs. Give each pair one of the dialogue exchanges or first and last lines provided and a few minutes to discuss how they might work with it. Then run a "goldfish bowl" activity where each pair performs their exchange in front of the class. Have the observers note down in their journals whether they found the exchange convincing or not. What advice could they provide to the pair which could improve the authenticity of the exchange?

- Spend time discussing with students the difference between the quality of the dialogue you might hear in a play and that which people have in everyday conversations. Explain that the words in a play have to move the story along.

Note: Some of these exchanges have a potential third character, so pairs will need to swap parts. The lines in "First and Last" might sometimes be spoken by the same person.

EXCHANGES

Exchange 1

a. Mom's out—let's have a look round her room.
b. She'll be mad if she finds out.

a. I wonder what she's bought me for my birthday. I hope it's not something to wear.
b. What's wrong with something to wear?

a. Well, it's not a proper present. I don't want anything useful unless it's a computer.
b. Don't be stupid. You know Mom can't afford a computer.

a. I'm going to look anyway. (*Opens door and creeps into room*) Look, there's a box. YAY! Let's try and open it.
b. No! Mom'll be back soon.

a. I'm just going to get it out of the box—that's all. This polystyrene is impossible to move. Got it!
b. I can hear Mom's car in the driveway!

a. Cripes. I can't get it back into the box!
(Now carry on the exchange.)

Exchange 2

a. So, how many times is it now?
b. I don't know.

a. I've counted four so far this term. Four times you've been sent to me.
b. Yes.

a. (*Looks through a folder*) Let's see, twice for extreme rudeness, once for tripping someone, and last week for defacing a poster on the classroom wall.
b. (*Silence*)

a. What is it this time—and, more to the point, why are you doing these things?
(Now carry on the exchange.)

Exchange 3

a. I want to return this pair of shoes. The sole is coming unstuck on both, and I only got them two weeks ago.
b. Have you worn them in the rain?

a. Yes, but the soles shouldn't come unstuck.
b. I'm sorry, but it looks as though you've been wading through water in them.

a. I certainly have not! Look, I'm not going to argue. I want a full refund on these shoes.
(Now carry on the exchange.)

Exchange 4

a. Look, Captain, it seems as though we're closer than we thought to the city of Axo.
b. Ah yes, there are the triple towers of the High Regency. Can you zoom in on the top floor of the second tower?

a. Zooming in now. It's not a very clear picture I'm afraid, Captain.
b. Clear enough for me to see that Lord Shandos is holding a meeting with the Bandits of Kraal.

a. What should we do now?
b. Can you fix me up a satellite voice-line to that visi-screen behind his head? I'd like to pay them an unexpected call.
(Now carry on the exchange.)

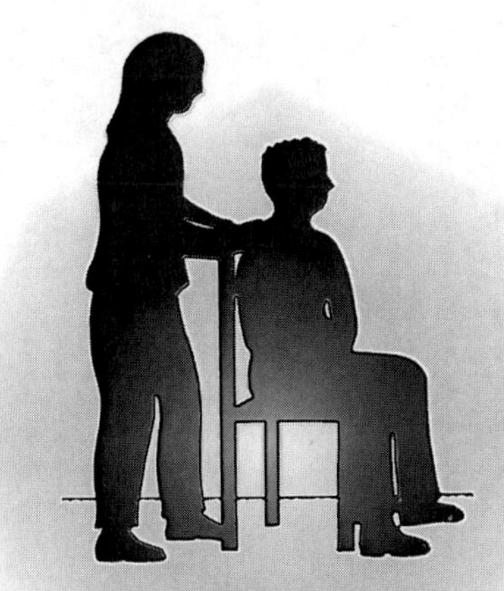

Exchange 5

a. Mom says I have to ask you if I can go out with my friends to a school party on Saturday.
b. No, you can't.

a. Why not?
b. Because you never tidy your room, you won't help out around the house and... you scraped the side of my car with your bike.

a. I did not!
b. Don't lie to me. I saw it when I went out to the garage this morning. You should have TOLD me. So you can forget any party.

a. I did NOT scrape your car...and anyway, you're not my REAL Dad, so you can't tell me what to do.
(Now carry on the exchange.)

Exchange 6

a. What's wrong?
b. I don't want to talk about it.

a. Tell me. I might be able to help.
b. Nobody can help.

b. If I tell you, do you promise not to tell a soul?
a. Of course.
(Now carry on the exchange.)

CREATIVE DRAMA

FIRST AND LAST LINES

First: Look, I know you don't like me, but there's something I have to tell you.
Last: I never knew.

First: That's the sixth cake you've eaten.
Last: You'd better be quick.

First: Sit down and have a drink.
Last: I know you won't believe me, but you'll get over it.

First: Don't keep looking over my shoulder.
Last: You mean to say you got an A and I got a C+?

First: I can't see where I'm going.
Last: Look out. HEEELLPP!!

First: I left it on the table.
Last: You took it!

First: Call the store manager.
Last: Don't let go of her.

First: Where does it hurt?
Last: We're going to have to take it out, I'm afraid.

First: Come on... let's see if we can get a free meal.
Last: Well, it worked last time.

First: I know the way.
Last: I knew you'd get us into a mess.

First: Put it up over here.
Last: Take it down, then!

First: When did you say this incident took place?
Last: I have no choice but to fine you.

First: What did you do with my CDs?
Last: How dare you!

First: This is your fault.
Last: I always put honey on mine!

First: I saw your dad's name in the newspaper.
Last: Please don't mention it to anyone.

First: Just pretend you didn't notice.
Last: You could at least apologize.

First: The sun's going down. Better light the campfire.
Last: Thanks for telling me... but I don't think I'll sleep very well now.

First: Thanks, it's really beautiful.
Last: Oh look, there's a huge crack.

First: You'll never guess who I saw kissing Kelly Dixon.
Last: Do you think we should tell her?

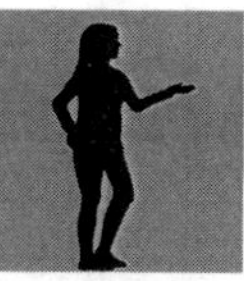

First: Which one shall we choose?
Last: Why are you always so greedy?

First: Gasp!
Last: My hero!

First: You can turn that rubbish off.
Last: When YOU pay the bills, YOU can make the decisions.

First: The opening's down here somewhere. We'll need to be quick to avoid the searchlight.
Last: That was close.

First: It's a disgrace; they ought to do something about it.
Last: I blame the government.

First: I haven't got quite enough money on me.
Last: But, I can't walk that far!

First: Look! There's Brad! Hi, Brad!
Last: How embarrassing.

First: Give it back, you nasty girl, or I'll tell my mommy!
Last: Mommy!

MORE FIRST AND LAST LINES

Following are some more first and last lines where the lines don't seem to immediately relate. Students must try and link the two statements in a short improvised scene. Give them thinking time first!

First: Is this your bag?
Last: Absolutely, I love spaghetti.

First: Flowers, how lovely.
Last: That was a rotten trick, you pig.

First: Where have you been?
Last: I always put chocolate icing on it.

First: I think I like the green one best.
Last: It must be poisonous.

First: My shoelace is knotted
Last: That's a huge fish.

First: What have you done to your hair?
Last: Put some glue on it.

First: It looks like a large hole.
Last: They are lovely and fresh.

First: We're entering a time warp.
Last: Thanks for the tea.

Published by Educational Impressions, Inc.

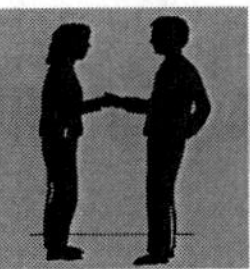

CREATIVE DRAMA

First: Did you see that flash?
Last: It was behind the door all the time.

First: Yes, I got the award as I expected.
Last: My leg's stuck.

First: She painted all the window frames purple.
Last: Well, switch it on then!

First: Fourteen, they said!
Last: The wheel fell off.

First: I hate you.
Last: I love you.

Here are two examples of how these first and last lines can be linked into a dialogue which at first seems to have no connection:

a. Is this your bag? I'll carry it for you.
b. I have another case to collect. Ah, here it is.

a. Just put it in the trunk. It isn't far to the house.
b. What lovely countryside. I think I'm going to enjoy my stay.

a. I do hope you will—here we are. Your room is here on the right.
b. What a pleasant room—and a beautiful view of the garden.

a. The bathroom is here through this door. You might like to freshen up. Come down when you're ready. I expect you're hungry.
b. I'm starving. Thank you. (Later)

a. You sit here. Help yourself to a drink. I hope you like Italian.
b. Absolutely, I love spaghetti.

a. Flowers, how lovely. How did you know it was my birthday?
b. You keep reminding me. How could I forget!

a. No, I didn't. Well, if I did, it wasn't because I wanted you to give me a present.
b. Oh, well, that's good because I pinched the flowers from our next-door neighbor's garden.

a. Well, you can take them back. I don't want stolen goods.
b. Only kidding! Why don't you smell them? They're gorgeous.

a. Oh, they stink! That was a rotten trick, you pig!

Published by Educational Impressions, Inc.

CREATIVE DRAMA

IMPROVISING IN PAIRS

The following story lines can be used with two characters as a way of building up to working in groups of 3 or more. Again, copy the pages onto card. Laminate them and cut them up.

- You have always felt you look very different from your parents and siblings. You are looking for a pen in your mother's desk when you come across an intriguing document. You open it and see that it is your Adoption Certificate! Your mother (or father) comes in and is angry at you for opening the desk. You are even angrier at what you see as their deception. Why did they always pretend you were their natural child?

- One of you is watching *Crimewatch* when the program shows a jeweler who has had valuable jewelry and watches stolen being interviewed. The hidden camera records the robbery and the thief looks exactly like the father of one of the students at your school. The next day that student is wearing a flashy gold watch and gold chains. What will you do? (The other student plays the person with the watch, etc.)

- You are siblings (brothers, sisters or sister/brother). One of you has been given a very expensive gold watch by her/his godmother for Christmas. The other sister/brother has been given a book by another godparent. Act out the conversation that occurs between you.

- One of you phones the other to borrow a sweater. After agreeing, the lender is annoyed to hear later that the borrower has had a party and the lender was not invited. When the party-giver returns the sweater, there is a horrible mark right down the front. You demand money for a new one. Dry cleaning is not a satisfactory option for you.

- The person sitting next to you in class is known to be "light fingered." One of the students tells the teacher her new pen is missing. The teacher tells the students to open their desks and bags. She finds the pen in your bag. The person who stole it must have slipped it in there! Try to prove your innocence.

- You are about to fly out of the country on a holiday. You need to go to the rest room. You ask your friend to watch your bags, etc. She/He decides to go and buy a magazine and leaves the bags for only a few minutes. When you both return to the spot, the bags have vanished. They contained your tickets, passport, travelers checks—everything! Confrontation! Consternation! How will you be able to take your holiday?

- You and your friend are on a safari in Africa. You reach a remote village. There is a roadblock. A menacing-looking soldier stops your vehicle and confiscates your passport, etc. You are put into a rondavel (African hut). What are you going to do? How heavily are you guarded? You have a spare set of keys. Can you escape?

- You are asked by a very friendly person sitting next to you on the plane if you could help her/him by carrying a small bag as she is laden. You happily do so. When you get to Customs, the "friend" disappears and the Customs Officer has asked you to open all the bags! What is in the extra bag? Help! Talk your way out of that one.

- One of you borrows a CD player from the other for a party. She/He assures you great care will be taken. It is returned next day. When the owner tries to play a CD on it, it jams. It is damaged! You phone your friend, who swears it was working perfectly at the party! How can you resolve this? You are very angry!

CREATIVE DRAMA

- As a medical student you have discovered a new substance that is a medical breakthrough to cure (your choice of a medical condition). When the results are published in a medical journal, you discover to your anger that the professor has taken all the credit. Confront her/him.

- You buy several small items from a store. You have given the shop owner a $100 bill you received for your birthday. When you get home, you check the change and find he/she has given you $10.00 short. You return to the store, but the owner says she/he is positive you had the correct change and that you ought to have checked it in the shop. You are really upset and point out you went straight home and straight back to the shop. Solution?

- You are strolling through a wooded area. You see a mound covered with leaves. You scrape off the leaves and find a large wooden box—a little like a coffin. You are struggling to open it when someone comes up behind you and demands to know what you are doing. He/She claims to own the box. The finder is highly suspicious. Can you get the "owner" to open the box and, if so, what is in it?'

- You are on a school trip to a city. You wander off alone and get lost. Where is everyone? A strange-looking man offers to show you a short cut back to the hostel. It is getting dark. What are your options?

- One of you is a new nurse and the other a doctor. A patient is brought in after an accident. The doctor operates and gives clear instructions to the nurse as to how much medication to inject. The nurse misunderstands and doubles the dose. The patient lapses into a coma. The doctor returns!

- One of you runs a clothes shop. The other is a customer. The customer takes several items to try on. There is not much room in the cubicle and one of the items drops into your tote! You gather the others and say they are not suitable, thank you. You leave the shop. The owner runs after you and accuses you of shoplifting! How can you explain the item in your tote?

IMPROVISING WITH A SET OF CHARACTERS AND A SITUATION

Another approach to improvisation is to provide a set of characters and a situation for groups of students to use. Try the ones following. Give the cards out and allow groups 15 minutes to prepare. They must establish their roles and run through the dialogue. Some of the situations need resolutions; in others the resolutions are provided, but it's not clear how they are achieved. Copy them onto card. Laminate them and cut them up.

Situation 1 *A group of elderly women in a rest home at dinner time*
The elderly women have been saying how they think they are being poisoned. They taste the food—it is bitter. They insist the matron eats with them.

Situation 2 *A group of students visit a chocolate factory*
They are shown around and warned not to lean over the vats or touch any switches. They can eat as much chocolate as they like. Several things go wrong. A student falls into a vat of chocolate. Another pulls a switch with disastrous results. Another eats too much chocolate.

Situation 3 *Parents take their twin babies to the photographer*
They will not stay still despite all the attempts of the photographer. The parents eventually tie them to chairs.

Situation 4 *The toy shop at midnight*
The toys come to life and talk about the rough treatment they get from their owners and plan revenge.

Situation 5 *A dog obedience class*
Some students are owners; others are the pets. One student is a frustrated instructor. The dogs finish the training session by fighting.

Situation 6 *Some muggers set upon an old lady*
She has been taking defense lessons and flattens them.

Situation 7 *Students and teacher on a visit to a museum*
Students observe someone taking a valuable Egyptian artifact.

Situation 8 *A posh dinner party and everything goes wrong.*
The host cannot open the wine and breaks the bottle. The soup is too salty. The dinner is far too spicy. The dessert is frozen solid. The maid spills hot coffee all over the guests.

Situation 9 *Search party*
A group set off to find a small child who has wandered into the forest. They eventually find him/her. She is injured. They make a stretcher and carry her out to safety.

Situation 10 *The laundromat*
One person is in charge. Various characters come in to use the machines. One puts in far too much soap powder. A child opens the door while the machine is working. Someone mixes up the whites and colors.

Situation 11 *A railway carriage*
A youth lights up. It is a no-smoking train.

Situation 12 *Moving*
Removal people and an agitated owner. Movers are inexperienced and find difficulty with everything including grand piano and delicate vases and valuable pictures.

Situation 13 *Building a house*
New builders on the job. Experienced foreman goes crazy as they drop bricks, smash glass, cut wood wrong length, and injure themselves and each other.

Situation 14 *The student teacher*
A student teacher is teaching a drama class. The teacher is being observed by her college supervisor. Some students try to make life difficult. Others want the teacher to do well in front of the supervisor.

Situation 15 *The hairdressers*
Hairdressers and clients. A parent is trying to get a reluctant four year old to have a hair cut. A woman is not sure what she wants done. A color has gone disastrously wrong. The phone won't stop ringing.

Situation 16 *The meter attendant*
A meter attendant marks tires of vehicles, eventually placing tickets on their windshields. Irate owners return and invent incredible excuses as to why they were not in time to recharge the meters.

Situation 17 *Baby-sitting*
Two friends are baby-sitting two toddlers. They have plans to watch videos and do some urgent homework. The toddlers are fast asleep when the parents go out, but within minutes wake up and won't go back to sleep. The friends try everything. The toddlers finally go to sleep just before the parents come home.

Situation 18 *Party*
Your parents are away overnight. They trust you and have said that you can have a few school friends around to watch videos and eat pizza. One friend brings someone you don't know. Before long this new person has called other people on a cell phone and soon everybody for miles around knows there's "a party" at your place. You are terrified that people that you don't know will trash your house. You have to act quickly.

Situation 19 *The trapeze artists*
You are a flamboyant family of Italian trapeze artists, brilliant and confident. You have been practicing a new and daring routine for the circus. The television people are there, the big top is packed, and the atmosphere is electric.

Situation 20 *The cave*
A group of students are caving. The passage gets narrower and narrower. There is a sudden shift of rock and the roof collapses, trapping some of the students. Others need to come up with a rescue plan.

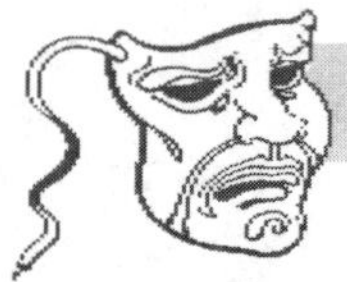

CREATIVE DRAMA

GENRE SITUATIONS

Most students who watch films and television have naturally internalized the codes and cues of a range of dramatic genre. Have some fun with the following stereotypical situations in groups, but first discuss as a class the typical dramatic features of the following genre. Discuss character types, typical plots, settings, creating the era: props, sound/visual effects, etc...

- **the doctor/nurse soap opera**
- **the Victorian melodrama**
- **the Agatha Christie-type murder mystery**
- **the horror/ghost story**
- **the science-fiction story**
- **the Western**

Students will need to think about playing these "straight," hamming it up or creating unexpected twists. Only the setting has been provided here. Groups will have to flesh the situations out with a plot and characters.

The Doctor/Nurse Soap Opera
The emergency room. A child has been brought in after being badly bitten by a dog.

The Victorian Melodrama
The drawing room of a rich landowner's house. He is planning how to get more rent from his farm workers.

The Agatha Christie-type Murder Mystery
A grand hotel. It is the 1930s. A famous writer has been discovered dead in the bath of her suite.

The Horror/Ghost Story
A castle in Eastern Europe. Two young travellers are lost on the mountain road. They drive to the castle to ask for directions.

The Science-Fiction Story
An unidentified flying object crash lands in the Australian desert. Two teenagers see it come down.

The Western
A packed saloon bar. Two feuding gunslingers are playing cards. At stake is a life.

FAIRY TALES, FABLES AND PROVERBS

Well-known stories can provide excellent material for improvisations even for very young students. The following are suggestions for varying ages:

- Snow White in the dwarves' cottage being visited by the Wicked Queen disguised as an old woman selling apples.
- An encounter between Red Riding Hood and the wolf when the latter is disguised as the grandmother.
- Cinderella's sisters getting ready for the ball.
- Jack bringing home the beans to his mother after "selling" the cow.
- When the Emperor is persuaded by the tailors to put on the invisible clothes.
- The conversation between the three little pigs and the wolf.
- Creation myths from ancient cultures. This could lead onto the devising of "new" creation myths like Why the Sky is Blue or How the (local geographical feature) Got There.

Aesop's Fables are an excellent source of improvisation too. Read the fable first to the students and then ask them to improvise the story. These are good ones:

- **The Wolf and the Goat**
- **The Cat and the Mice**
- **The Fox and the Grapes**
- **The Wolf and the Crane**
- **The Hare and the Tortoise**

Proverbs are seldom used by teachers for improvisation (or mime) but they can be the basis of some fine dramatic incidents. Students could try and work out what the proverb is that another group is performing. Spend some time beforehand explaining what a proverb is (i.e., a pithy distillation of some human truth). Try these:

- **A stitch in time saves nine.**
- **Many hands make light work.**
- **A friend in need is a friend indeed.**
- **Too many cooks spoil the broth.**
- **Pride goes before a fall.**
- **Look before you leap.**

CHARADES

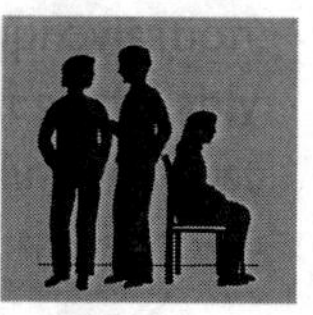

Compound words are a never-ending source of improvisation. The charade can be acted out by one student, but preferably two or more. One student can enact a scene, hiding the first part of the word; the second student can act out the second part of the word; and together they can act out the whole word. There is considerable ingenuity in hiding the word in the dialogue. Students watching can be given a limited time or number of questions to guess the full word. Some suggestions are:

Butter-fly	**Ice-cream**	**Night-dress**	**Sun-shine**
Rose-bud	**Lip-stick**	**Foot-stool**	**Candle-stick**
Sun-set	**Hair-brush**	**Rain-bow**	**Paint-brush**
Prim-rose	**Walking-stick**	**Lolly-pop**	**Pen-knife**
Foot-path	**Shoe-lace**	**Straw-berry**	**Wash-basin**

TITLES

More advanced students will enjoy the challenge of improvising a short play from a title given by the teacher. This requires time to prepare—at least ten to fifteen minutes should be given. It is ideal for classroom teaching as the title(s) can be given a week in advance and the students can get together during the week. The results can be extremely innovative and entertaining.

Some suggested titles are:

Mrs. Bradley's Secret	**The Accident**
The Kidnappers	**First-Night Nerves**
Family Troubles	**Teacher's Pet**
The Cheat	**Behind the Locked Door**
The Boy with Ginger Hair	**The Interview**
The New Girl	**Missing**
The Wonder Brain	**The Reading of the Will**
The Birthday Surprise	**The Midnight Call**
Aunty's Win	**The Committee Meeting**
The Worst Day Ever	**The Drowning**
Secrets	**The Hidden Key**
The Gypsy Fortuneteller	**Secret Passage**
The School Dance	**Heirloom**
A Stranger Calls	**Finders, Keepers**
The Bully	**Dad's Shock**

POSTBOX IMPROVISATIONS

Prepare three mailboxes (plastic ice-cream containers are excellent) and mark one "Settings," the second "Characters," and the third "Props." Ask each student to take one card from each box and create a situation in the setting named, acting the part of the character named, visualizing or utilizing the imaginary prop named on the card. Try these:

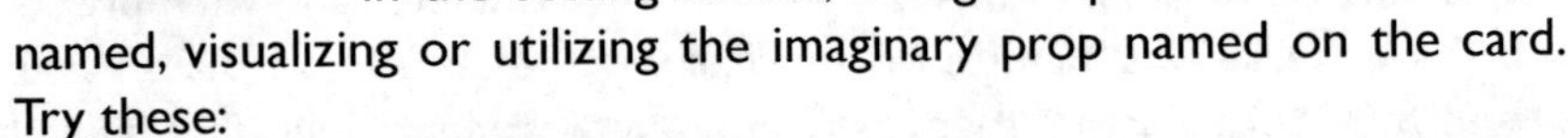

SETTINGS	CHARACTERS	PROPS
A sports field	Police officer	Telephone
An elevator	Surfer	Eggs
The airport	Gang member	Basket
Classroom	Spy	Candle
The mall	Vampire	A sandwich
A coach	Clown	Picnic basket
The zoo	Teacher	Encyclopedia
The park	Driving instructor	Video camera
The beach	Juggler	Diamond necklace
A kitchen	Postal worker	Ice cream
A train	An alien	Tomato sauce

The combinations of this exercise are endless!

NOTE: Students may prefer to create a scene the first time with another student, or even the teacher, playing opposite him/her.

PROPS

Placing props in the middle of the floor can help a student become a character (e.g., a scarf can make a gypsy, a baby, a dancer, an old woman, a pirate, etc). A stick can be a wand, a gun, a pointer, a hammer, etc. Masks, wigs, cloaks and other costumes give added fun to improvisations.

As students gain in confidence it is a good idea to help them act out their improvisation within a time slot; for example, two minutes. It is more difficult to do satisfying work in such a short time, but as long as the scene has an introduction, a middle and a satisfying conclusion, then two minutes is often all the time that will be available in a large class.

PROVIDING FEEDBACK

After completion of any improvisation allow time for discussion. These questions will help to guide the discussion. Was it easy to follow the mime or improvisation? Was the character(s) believable? Was movement natural—did anyone walk through the "table"? Was the dialogue clear and convincing? Was there a satisfactory climax? What other ways could the scene have been played or improved?

INTRODUCING MIME

Mime is the art of creating the illusion of reality. In order to communicate fully with the audience, the performer has to convey the world around him/her as well as an inner world—thoughts, feelings, desires, needs. The mime must clearly show what emotions the performer has and then the resolution.

Even young students can be taught to simulate hunger, fatigue, fear, anticipation, cold, etc., and then proceed to create the scene which deals with these sensations. Mime involves learning the ability to isolate various parts of the body with total control and then coordinating them as needed. Shy students who find difficulty in creating dialogue often find it easier to begin with mime. As they grow in confidence, the same situation can be re-enacted adding conversation to turn it into an improvisation.

Before starting a mime class, it is a good idea to practice some relaxation exercises and then physical exercises (or mimes) that will loosen up the arms, legs, head and torso. Children are naturally supple, but some older students need these exercises to avoid stiff movements instead of the fluid ones necessary.

EXERCISES FOR FEET AND LEGS

- **Mime skipping**
- **Jump like a kangaroo**
- **Leap like a frog**
- **Lie on your back and "bicycle"**
- **Point to items in the room using toes**
- **Creep like a mouse**
- **Walk through thick mud**
- **Leap from stone to stone**
- **Tiptoe up the stairs**
- **Sashay down a catwalk**

EXERCISES FOR THE HEAD AND NECK

- **Mime a giraffe reaching for the highest leaf**
- **Look left, right, left, right crossing the road**
- **Watch a tennis match**
- **Be a puppet worked by invisible hands**
- **Watch a plane moving across the sky**

EXERCISES FOR THE TORSO

- **Be an inflatable rubber toy**
- **Wriggle across the floor like a snake**
- **Be a tree bending in a cyclone**
- **Rotate from the hips like a windmill**

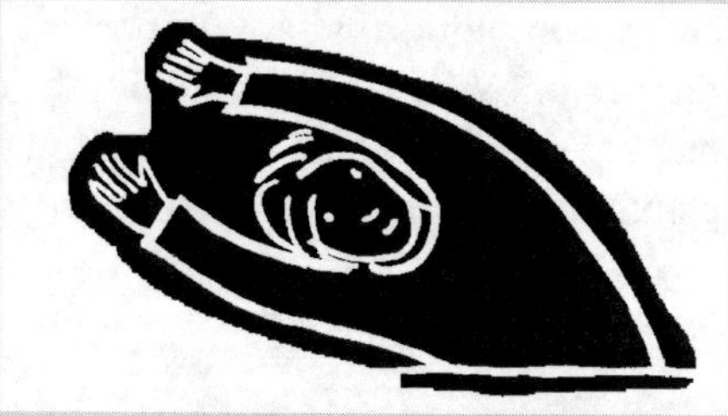

Published by Educational Impressions, Inc.

EXERCISES FOR THE HANDS AND ARMS

- **Wave goodbye to a friend**
- **Hang out the washing**
- **Flutter like a bird hovering over its nest**
- **Smooth some suntan lotion on your arms**
- **Wash your face and hands**
- **Pound clay ready to do some modeling**
- **Make an elaborate flower arrangement**

Students should start out in miming by doing very simple everyday actions such as:

- **washing the face and hands**
- **brushing hair**
- **putting on socks and shoes**
- **getting dressed**
- **pouring cereal into a bowl**
- **making a cup of tea**
- **opening a can of soda**
- **making a sandwich**
- **getting on a bicycle and getting off again**
- **purchasing something from a shop**
- **writing a letter**
- **making a telephone call**

These are things we do every day without being aware of how we do them.

When they have mastered these simple mimes, they could try more elaborate ones. The student must at all times be aware of the significance of every movement. Fluttery, small gestures are out.

WORKING AS AN INDIVIDUAL

SHOWING EMOTION

The face is the mirror of the soul, and the next step is to use it to show emotion. Start with simple exercises to show:

Give each a context. For example, for "fear" you could say, "Show on your face how you would feel if you were doing a parachute jump and your chute doesn't open up."

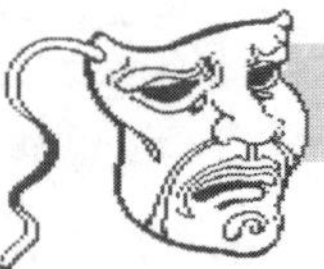

CREATIVE DRAMA

Tell students that the feelings must come from within and be expressed in the face and eyes without moving any other part of the body. Then bring other parts of the body in with these mimes:

- **Go for a walk with your dog. You meet a friend. You are so pleased to see her. She has some sad news to relate. Comfort her.**
- **Go to a restaurant with a friend. You are paying. She or he orders the most expensive items on the menu.**
- **You are very tired. You go to the beach, blow up your float, lay on it and just relax with the warmth of the sun on your body. Suddenly the tide comes in.**
- **Look into a mirror. You are worried about the way you look.**

Small Hand Movements

Have students mime picking up from the floor the following items:

A needle and thread
A squashed tomato
A wriggling, affectionate puppy
A handful of ice cubes
A diamond ring
A broken egg
A pin
A broken necklace
A ladybird
A basket with a baby in it
An injured bird
A pile of twigs
A tiny glove

Now ask them to build a small situation around each one. For example, what might they be doing with the needle and thread? Sewing up a hole in a sock? Finishing off the hem of a gown for a rich person?

Facial Movements

Have students eat the following:

A lemon-meringue pie
An ice-cream cone on a hot day
An enormous hamburger
A juicy orange
A bunch of grapes
A strong cheese
A cup of soup
A sour apple
A chocolate éclair
A banana
Hot curry
An ice cube
A very hard toffee
A bowl of corn flakes
A very hot cup of tea
Spaghetti

Now ask them to create a setting for each one. For example, where is the lemon-meringue pie being eaten: at a party, in a restaurant, in Italy? What happens next?

Whole-Body Movements

Have students move in the manner of the following:

An elderly person
A crawling baby
A large person
A hungry person
A cold person
A lazy person
A thin person
A miserable person
A naughty person
A stuck-up person
An excited person
An inquisitive person
A suspicious person
A sly person
A boisterous person
An unhappy person

Now build these people into real characters and create a situation which transforms them. For example, what could transform the cold person? Does the sun come out? Are you given a warm coat? Do you build a fire?

Characterization and Role-Playing

These can be introduced when students build a bit more confidence. The important thing to remember is to STAY IN ROLE. For example, when a student plays the part of an elderly person, it is important to remain in character all the time. It is no good tottering unsteadily across the room and then bouncing onto a chair. An elderly person would slowly lower him/herself down.

Remind students that mouths are to remain firmly closed. All sense of the character comes from movement only.

Various occupations can provide material for characterizations.

- **Weight lifter**
- **Butcher**
- **Cinema usher**
- **Nurse**
- **Dentist**
- **Zookeeper**
- **Hairdresser**
- **Burglar**
- **Skater**
- **House-painter**
- **Photographer**
- **Plumber**
- **Concert pianist**
- **Shoplifter**
- **Waitress**
- **Opera singer**
- **Magician**
- **New teacher**
- **Department-store demonstrator**
- **Flight attendant**
- **Checkout clerk**
- **Rubbish collector**

Having established how the character might be portrayed in his/her occupation, students could now create a scene and think of the many situations this character would find him/herself in. For example, the weightlifter, heaving, struggling, finally gets the weights above his/her head, then tips over backwards.

Published by Educational Impressions, Inc.

When students need to create the impression of another person, they will need to practice this imaginary interaction. They could try "hearing" knocking on a door, opening the door, showing someone into a room and introducing him/her to someone else.

Students could observe each other and give feedback on how well the "invisible" person is being realized. They might want to walk through the actual movements in pairs first. For the mime, movements will need to be more precisely realized and larger than life. Spend time practicing how to mime the presence of inanimate objects like the opening and closing of doors, the moving of a chair, looking into a mirror, etc.

NOTES:
When practicing mime, it is a good idea to have a full-length mirror available. "Walking" can be done "on the spot" if space is limited.

Ask students to carefully observe their hand and arm movements, putting themselves in the place of the audience. Would the audience have any difficulty in understanding what they are doing?

WORKING WITH A PARTNER

Mime becomes more difficult when individuals start working with a partner or partners. If groups are creating a scene, every movement must be carefully choreographed. There is no point in several people waving their arms around. They may know what they are doing but the audience won't have a clue. Individuals should start by working with only one partner first and becoming familiar with this way of working before attempting a larger scene.

Here are some ideas for pairs to try:

The nanny and the lost toddler
The taxi driver and the drunk
The explorer and the mummy
The hypnotist and the audience member
Two people waiting for a late bus
The photographer and the fussy bride
The recently arrived alien and the farmer
The difficult customer and the waitress
The boy and the bad dog
The window dresser and the passerby
The dentist and the frightened patient
The director and the movie star
The first date
The driving test
The parent and the child who won't eat
The enthusiastic ballroom dancer and the novice

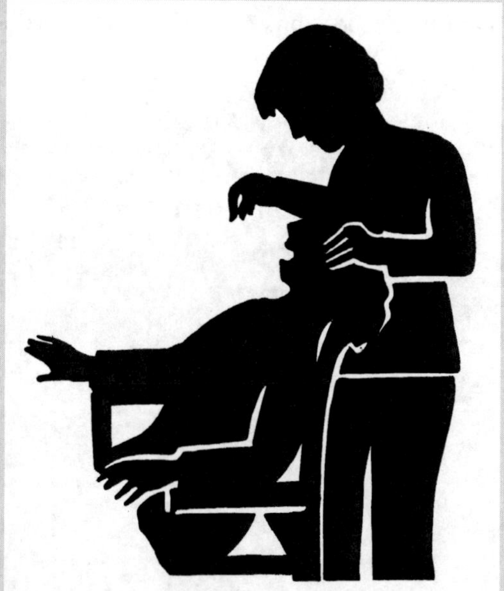

ANIMALS

Discuss animal movements and behavior as a class. In groups have students mime the following animals:

- **Birds looking for food. A cat lurks close by**
- **Giraffes eating from trees**
- **Big cats eating a carcass**
- **Monkeys eating bananas**
- **A family of elephants moving towards a watering hole**
- **A troupe of performing Jack Russells**
- **Dressage horses**
- **Stalked deer**
- **Seals sunbathing**
- **Hippos having a mud bath**
- **Fish feeding frenzy**

MIME IDEAS

What to do next? Coming up with ideas for individuals, pairs and groups is always a problem, so the following pages contain many ideas of varying difficulty for students to attempt. They are mostly directed at individuals, but can easily be extended to include others. Remember, the mimes can be turned into improvisations and the improvisations into mimes. Just remove speech, be very conscious of movement, and create an imaginary world for the audience. Have fun! Copy them onto card, laminate them and cut them into strips.

- **Making your first parachute jump.**
- **Changing the tires on a truck in the pouring rain.**
- **Making and tossing pancakes.**
- **Build a treehouse. A gale-force wind starts blowing.**
- **A do-it-yourself chair-making kit. Try sitting on it.**
- **Cleaning the windows on the thirteenth floor. What is going on inside and below?**
- **A visit to the dentist. He has an enormous injection needle and you react badly to it.**
- **Mending a leak in the water bed.**
- **Coming home late after a party. Try not to wake everyone.**

CREATIVE DRAMA

- Finding a snake in your luggage.
- Sailing for the first time.
- Going on a blind date.
- Making a cup of tea in a tent.
- Mixing concrete for the first time.
- Cleaning out the parakeet's cage—after three months.
- Taking a bath when the phone rings—again and again.
- Tuning the piano—what is causing that strange noise?
- Cleaning filthy soccer cleats.
- Choosing a bunch of flowers.
- Painting a picture. Is there a model?
- Baby-sitting for the first time.
- Climbing the Himalayas. Landslide.
- Cruising down the river—your boat leaks.
- In a china shop with a small child.
- Make an origami bird or animal. It becomes alive.
- At sea in a gale.
- In a haunted house.
- Out in a thunderstorm—shelter under a tree.

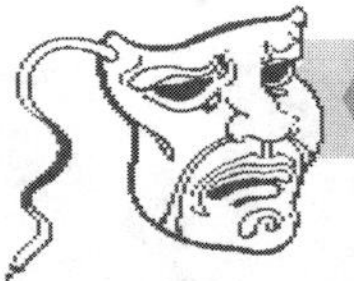

CREATIVE DRAMA

- Wallpaper for the first time.
- You pick up your new eyeglasses. You are given the wrong ones.
- You have to exit on stage. The door sticks.
- You get ready for a party. Your zipper gets stuck.
- You are out to dinner. The meat is very, very tough.
- You try to put up a tent in a howling gale.
- Make a cake—you put in salt instead of sugar.
- Asleep in bed. Something is crawling on your pillow.
- You try to crack a nut with your teeth. You break two teeth.
- Try to get down from a camel or an elephant.
- You try to glue a broken vase together. You end up by gluing yourself to it.
- You help move a baby grand piano—up stairs!
- You are singing in an opera. Your voice goes.
- You find a bottle washed up on the shore. There is a message inside.
- You accidentally drop a match near a box of fireworks. They go up.
- You make toffee—taste it. Your teeth stick together.
- Peel an orange. The juice keeps going into your eyes.
- You want to know what is in your mother's desk, but it is locked. Force it open.
- Get a book from the library. You settle down to read it. You open the first page and an enormous, black, hairy spider creeps out.

CREATIVE DRAMA

- You bake and ice a cake as a surprise for your mother. The icing is too runny and keeps rolling off.
- You go to fetch the milk from the milkbox. It has been stolen by the boy next door again. This time you confront him.
- You wear your new shoes. They get tighter and tighter and you end up in agony.
- You have written a poem for a competition. You receive a check for $100.00.
- You are asleep in bed. You wake and smell something burning—is the house on fire or is it your electric blanket?
- You are excited about the outdoor sports competition as you have been training hard. You wake to find it pouring rain.
- You are happily soaking in the bath when there is a huge earthquake.
- You are at sea in a small boat. There is a violent thunderstorm. You do not have a life jacket.
- Your friend lives on the 23rd floor of a high-rise building. You are scared of heights. She invites you out onto the balcony.
- You are in the woods and go for a picnic by the water. What are those eyes speeding towards you in the river?
- Paint a picture. The phone rings. When you return, the dog has walked all over it.
- Drink a fizzy drink—it goes right up your nose.
- Stroke a kitten—it has fleas.
- Eat a huge burger with lettuce, tomato and cheese. The filling shoots out onto someone's lap!
- Polish a table. You can't get the marks out. You rub off the varnish!
- Put on a very cozy coat. What is inside the pockets?
- Walk barefoot on hot sands.
- Try the sea water—it is icy cold.
- Walk on a swing bridge—someone shakes it at the other end.

- Pick an apple and bite it—there is half a worm in it.
- Paddle your canoe in rough water. Is that a waterfall ahead?
- Go to bed at camp—someone has put a frog in your bed.
- Comb your hair—it is full of knots.
- Peel an onion—it makes you cry.
- Sweep the floor—the dust makes you sneeze.
- Take a baby for a walk. Everyone stops to admire it.
- Catch an enormous fish. Can you land it?
- Walk your dog. It keeps chasing other dogs.
- Someone tries to snatch your bag—fight him/her off.
- Swallow disgusting medicine. Is it the right bottle?
- Take the top off a boiled egg. It smells awful.
- Unwrap a very sticky candy—you cannot get off all the paper.
- Type a letter. You keep making mistakes.
- Pick some flowers—you are stung.
- You are sitting under a tree—a snake slithers down it.
- Polish your new shoes—the heel or sole comes off one.
- Write a letter—your pen dries up and you cannot find another.
- Open a bottle of champagne—it explodes and drenches you.

CREATIVE DRAMA

- Clean your teeth—one of them falls out.
- Put up wallpaper. When you have finished and stand back, you find it's upside down.
- Paint a door. Unexpectedly someone opens it and slams it onto you and your clothes.
- Get undressed and into bed—there is a rat at the foot of the bed.
- Take a shower—the water turns freezing suddenly.
- Make a cake—it looks beautiful when you lift it out of the oven. You drop it.
- Unwrap a parcel from your grandmother while she watches—you do not like the present inside.
- Shell an Easter egg—it is full of ants.
- You come in to wash your greasy hands—you cannot find the soap.
- You are on the bus. You notice a poisonous spider on the neck of the person in front of you.
- Put on clown or stage make-up. Look in the mirror—you get a fright.
- It is the day of your party—wake up and look in the mirror. You are covered with spots!
- You go in a plane for the first time. It is a bumpy ride.
- You dye your hair—it turns out green!
- Play the piano at a concert—the piano stool collapses.
- Sharpen a pencil—it keeps breaking. In the end you are left with a tiny stump.
- You make yourself a cup of tea—you absentmindedly put in salt instead of sugar.
- You bend to pick up a book—your glasses fall off and break.
- On your way home you hear a meowing—it turns out to be a baby tiger.

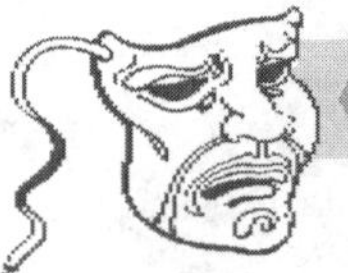

CREATIVE DRAMA

- You are lying in bed when you hear a strange lapping sound. You look out of the window—the water has flooded up to your window sill.
- You are playing ball—you break your neighbor's window.
- You see a sweet-looking kitten. You pick it up to stroke it—it scratches you right down your arm.
- You polish your black shoes. You do not remove all the polish and it goes all over the cream carpet.
- You are sweeping the classroom floor—you find a $100 bill!
- You decide to trim your hair yourself—you keep getting it uneven—it gets shorter and shorter.
- You come home very late from a party—try to climb the squeaky stairs without anyone hearing you.
- You are in a theater—you are hungry and your stomach starts to loudly rumble.
- You are watching TV when you hear a thud on the roof. You investigate.
- Walk on stones across a swiftly flowing river. You run out of stones!
- Visit the dentist—he removes the wrong tooth.
- Make a double-decker sandwich—you cut your hand badly.
- You check your lottery ticket—you have won first prize.
- You creep downstairs in the middle of the night to get something to eat from the fridge. Suddenly a hand descends on your shoulder.
- Shop in the supermarket. You absentmindedly pick up something and put it in your pocket. Someone sees you.
- You try to hammer a large nail into a box. You hit your hand instead.
- You are a dinner guest. You are eating your meal when you see the lettuce move across your plate.
- You unconsciously snag a thread of your best sweater on a wire fence. You keep walking and find you have unraveled the whole sweater!
- You are lying on your back in the sea lazily floating. Suddenly you see a shark's fin coming towards you.

CREATIVE DRAMA

- You are at a school assembly—you get an attack of hiccups.
- Blow up a large tube. You collapse with the effort.
- You are taken to an Italian restaurant and given a large plate of very long spaghetti and a fork. Try and eat it.
- Try getting into a wet suit. It is too small.
- You try to hang a picture on the wall. You just can't seem to get it straight.
- Pick some raspberries. You keep eating them. Suddenly you get a violent stomachache.
- You drop your keys down the gutter. Try and get them up.
- You are walking along the street. Suddenly there is an enormous earthquake and the sidewalk begins to separate.
- You come home and find you have been burgled.
- Try to thread a large piece of cotton into a tiny needle.
- You are at the beach. You lose a contact lens in the sand.
- You open a strangely shaped birthday gift.
- You discover there is an attic in your new house—explore.
- You are dared to go bungy-jumping. Is it safe?
- You come down to breakfast and find your dog has had six puppies.
- You badly need glasses—go to the optician—you cannot even see the board.
- Flop down on a beanbag chair. It bursts and all the beans roll out.
- You go to buy a new hat to wear to a wedding. You try on all shapes and sizes but can't decide.
- You have a new puppy. You discover it has chewed up your best shoes.

CREATIVE DRAMA

- You are late for an appointment and are waiting for the bus. When it comes, it is full and sails straight past you.
- You are knitting. Your new kitten plays with the wool and tangles it up. Try to unravel it.
- You are a balloon. Someone tries to blow you up. You burst.
- You are a puppet with a broken string—someone tries to mend you.
- Try to juggle—you keep dropping the balls at first—then...
- You make a wish—and it comes true.
- You are shelling peas. You find a gigantic slug in one pod—open the rest very cautiously.
- Open a cupboard—you find everything has been stolen.
- Someone gives you a $100 bill for no reason.
- You see a suspicious-looking character down an alley. You investigate.
- You nosily read a letter on your mother's desk. The contents give you a shock!
- You can hardly get into your untidy bedroom. Friends are coming—do a good job of tidying it up. You find all manner of lost treasures.
- You are walking when you hear a shot. Investigate.
- You are going for a walk. You look at the sky and decide not to take an umbrella. As you go further, it suddenly starts to pour.
- Take a seat. Open your case. Take out a musical instrument and start to play it. It needs tuning.
- Walk through a thick fog. You are nervous as you cannot see your hand in front of you. Is that a hole in the ground ?
- Gather sticks; build a fire and light it. A wind starts up.
- Pick up and comfort a small child whose toy has broken. Try and mend it.
- You are in the desert looking for water. Is that a mirage?

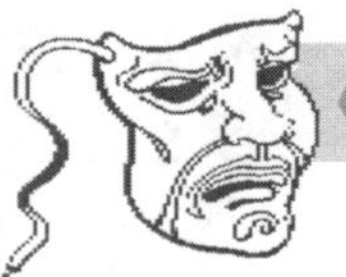

CREATIVE DRAMA

- You are an elderly person in a rest home. You taste your food. It has a bad taste. You want better food!
- You are in the mall and see a famous TV star signing autographs. You really want one.
- You are exploring a jungle. Your progress is slow. It is hot and there are lots of bugs.
- A person you have a crush on walks into the coffee shop.
- You crash-land on a planet. You step out of your craft into a strange world.
- You're surfing the Net. You strike up a "conversation" in a chat room.
- Buds are breaking into flower under a hot sun.
- Toys coming alive at midnight.
- Trees are being lashed by strong gale.
- A cook is preparing an apple pie. Who is that at the door? Where is the pie?
- A shoemaker is mending shoes. They start moving of their own accord.
- A blacksmith is shoeing a horse. It is high-spirited.
- A hairdresser is cutting long hair. Not that SHORT!
- A dentist is drilling teeth. Ouch, the injection doesn't work!
- A surgeon is performing an operation (first time).
- A patient is taking his/her first steps after an operation.
- First day at school. You need a friend.
- In a new house you find a small locked door. What is beyond it?
- You find a dead body in a field.

CREATIVE DRAMA

- You are driving a car for the first time. Where is the brake?
- You try to swallow your gum when spoken to by the teacher.
- Tight-rope walkers in a circus.
- Prisoner(s) escaping.
- You are escaping from a burning ship. There are not enough lifeboats.
- Old people in a home suddenly get up and dance. The director returns.
- The boys' school and girls' school get together for dance practice before the ball.
- Lost in a maze. There MUST be a way out!
- A sack race. What is in that sack?
- Painting a fence. Whose face is that?
- Building a large snowman.
- Catching butterflies. Look out for that ditch!
- Putting on clown make-up, then juggling.
- Shopping in a supermarket—your child starts screaming!
- Going up the Alps in a chair lift—it stops in mid air.
- Helping a victim at the scene of an accident.
- You decorate a room. What has happened to the door?
- Make a dog kennel. Persuade the unwilling dog to go in it.
- You spring-clean the house. What is at the back of the cupboard?

CREATIVE DRAMA

- You paint the roof—it is high and steep. Look out.
- You're five years old. You're meeting Santa Claus for the first time at the department store.
- You dress a shop window. The manikins come alive.
- You make a bookcase for a specific place. It doesn't fit.
- You build a house with cards. Who opened the door?
- Building a canoe. There must have been a hole in the wood.
- You find out that your son/daughter has been stealing from you.
- You make toffee apples. How do you get your teeth out?
- You build a doll house. Make and place furniture.
- You weed the garden—you discover something surprising.
- Hallowe'en—you knock at one door and get a nasty "trick."
- You set up a cake stand—nobody buys. You eat them yourself.
- You complain in a restaurant about the poor food and service.
- Explain directions to a foreign person who speaks no English.
- Rescue someone drowning.
- Nervous rabbits steal carrots from the farmer's field.
- You approach a fierce dog. That was your lunch!
- You shop in a supermarket. You spend too much. Put back several items without being seen.
- Cleaning windows, you see someone inside the room being attacked.

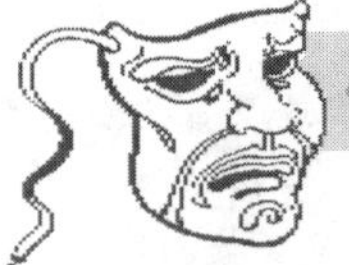

CREATIVE DRAMA

- You are a goalkeeper. Try stopping the opposition from scoring a goal.
- You hear a noise coming from the other side of a wall. Listen and try to track it down.
- You eat a banana and throw away the skin. An old lady slips on it.
- There is a knock at the door. There is a frightened neighbor on the doorstep.
- You try to remove the lid from a jar. It is stuck. It finally comes off and the contents spill over you.
- You are in a room when the ceiling starts coming down and the walls move in.
- You go to the shop and leave your bicycle outside. When you come out, you see someone riding it off into the distance.
- You are at a refined dinner party. You sit on an antique Queen Anne chair. It breaks and you crash to the floor.
- You hose the garden. A leak appears and the water goes all over you, soaking you.
- Put on a space suit and walk on the moon.
- You watch a horror film. You hear a noise outside!
- You answer the door to a traveling salesperson. You do not want anything, but he/she will not go away.
- You are at the cinema. Two people in front keep obscuring your view. You eventually get mad.
- You open your front door—there is a large basket on the doorstep—something is moving inside.
- You are delighted to finish a difficult jigsaw puzzle. There is a piece missing.
- Sit on a park bench—try to engage a member of the opposite sex in conversation—you are rejected.
- You bake a beautiful cake—you go to answer the phone. When you come back, your cat is eating it.
- You try to set a rat trap. It is very difficult. You snap it on your fingers.
- You are not looking where you are going. You walk into a lamppost.

CREATIVE DRAMA

- You try to find your seat in a pitch-black cinema. You have an ice-cream cone in your hand. Disastrous.
- You creep into a room and search for something. You hear someone coming and hide behind the curtains. The person goes to draw the curtains.
- You try to ice skate for the first time.
- It is night and as you walk past a jeweler's shop, the alarm bell goes off.
- It is your first attempt at using a pottery wheel. The clay goes everywhere.
- You are off to a dinner party. You try to tie a bow tie for the first time.
- It is pouring rain. You run from school to unlock your bike but have forgotten the combination.
- You arrive home—the key is missing from its usual hiding place. You search everywhere. Is there someone in the house?
- It is your birthday party. Everyone brings you presents you don't like. You are very disappointed until the last guest arrives. Then ...
- You go outside to investigate a noise. You hear someone moving in the bushes. You hit him on the head. It is a police officer!

EXTENSION

GIVE US A CLUE

This popular game is an excellent way of teaching mime—students usually become so involved in getting their message across they become totally unselfconscious. Students can think up their own titles but the teacher can provide extra cards with the titles of books, films, plays, songs, and TV programs and give them to the students to mime.

A time limit can be set. The students need instruction on how to show to their audience the number of words in the title (fingers held up); number of syllables in a word (fingers laid on arm); the word "The" (one finger laid on top of another); a small word (two fingers held close together); the whole word (hand circling the head) and "sounds like" (tugging the ear lobe).